NEW YORK REVIEW
CLASSICS

WATER

RUMI (Jalāl ad-Dīn Mohammad Balkhy, called Molana; 1207–1273), was born in or near the city of Balkh, in present-day Afghanistan. His father, an Islamic theologian, instructed him in prayer and fasting rituals while encouraging his studies in literature, science, and theology. When he was eleven, Rumi and his family left Balkh ahead of Mongol invaders, beginning a decade-long journey across Central Asia that ended in present-day Turkey. Following in his father's footsteps, Rumi became Konya's most eminent preacher and theologian. In 1244, he left behind his prodigious career to befriend the mystic vagabond Shams of Tabriz, his guide into the heart of Sufism. Ignited by Shams's teachings and by their ecstatic, tumultuous friendship, Rumi found his poetic voice. Considered the greatest poet of the Persian language, Rumi's major works are the *Masnavi*, a six-volume collection of mystical teachings in rhyming couplets, and the *Divan-e Shams-e Tabrizi*, a collection of lyric poetry dedicated to his spiritual mentor. He died and was buried in Konya. Around 1318, the historian Aflaki wrote Rumi's biography, drawing from Rumi's letters, the writings of Rumi's father and son, Shams's lectures, and interviews with surviving companions, leaving us a plethora of information about the thirteenth-century sage.

HALEH LIZA GAFORI is an Iranian American translator, performance artist, poet, and musician born in New York City. Her work has been published by *Harvard Review*, *The Brooklyn Rail*, Columbia University Press, and others. A recipient of a MacDowell fellowship and an NYSCA grant, she presents the poetry of Rumi at universities and institutions, including Stanford University, Lincoln Center, and the Academy of American Poets. Her first collection of Rumi translations, *Gold*, is also published by NYRB Classics.

WATER

RUMI

*Translated from the Persian and with
an introduction by*

HALEH LIZA GAFORI

NEW YORK REVIEW BOOKS

New York

THIS IS A NEW YORK REVIEW BOOK
PUBLISHED BY THE NEW YORK REVIEW OF BOOKS
207 East 32nd Street, New York, NY 10016
www.nyrb.com

Library of Congress Cataloging-in-Publication Data
Names: Jalāl al-Dīn Rūmī, Maulana, 1207–1273, author. | Gafori, Haleh Liza,
    translator.
Title: Water / by Rumi; translated by Haleh Liza Gafori.
Description: New York: New York Review Books, 2025. | Series: New York
    Review Books classics |
Identifiers: LCCN 2024039879 (print) | LCCN 2024039880 (ebook) |
    ISBN 9781681379166 (paperback) | ISBN 9781681379173 (ebook)
Subjects: LCSH: Jalāl al-Dīn Rūmī, Maulana, 1207–1273—Translations into
    English. | LCGFT: Poetry.
Classification: LCC PK6480.E5 G34 2025 (print) | LCC PK6480.E5 (ebook) |
    DDC 891/.5511—dc23/eng/20240921
LC record available at https://lccn.loc.gov/2024039879
LC ebook record available at https://lccn.loc.gov/2024039880

ISBN 978-1-68137-916-6
Available as an electronic book; ISBN 978-1-68137-917-3

The authorized representative in the EU for product safety and
compliance is eucomply OÜ, Pärnu mnt 139b-14, 11317 Tallinn, Estonia,
hello@eucompliancepartner.com, +33 757690241.

Printed in the United States of America on acid-free paper.
10 9 8 7 6 5 4 3 2 1

CONTENTS

INTRODUCTION

I FIRST heard the poetry of Molana Rumi when I was a child star-
ing out at the Hudson River from an eighth-floor apartment in New
Jersey. My father was reciting a poem about the *mastaan*—the Love-
drunk—tearing off their chains, or "mind-forg'd manacles" as William
Blake would say. The meanings eluded me at the time, but the propulsive,
muscular rhythms of the original Persian text left their impression.
My parents were young doctors who had emigrated from Iran to
America with one suitcase of clothing and two suitcases of books,
among them, a 1936 edition of the *Masnavi*, Rumi's vast book of
narrative and didactic poetry, handed down from my grandfather.
Eventually they would host monthly poetry nights, a Persian tradition
called *shab e sher*. Friends would come over and recite poetry in rounds
till the wee hours of the morning. I was one of the children on the
fringes, listening in, having no idea that Rumi would become a com-
panion for life. Looking back, I see the medieval sage and mystic's
verses as a luminous antidote to the bewildering materialism of
American life. Looking around at our warring and ecologically dev-
astated world, I hear them as urgent calls to reconsider the ways we
treat each other and our world. Always, I hear the beauty, tenderness,
exhilaration, and care that suffuse his poetry.

Water is my second volume of translations of Rumi's poetry, fol-
lowing *Gold*, and like *Gold*, it is drawn almost entirely from Rumi's
collection of lyric poetry, the *Divan-e Shams-e*, which contains more
than 3,200 ghazals and quatrains. Like *Gold* as well, *Water* comprises
fifty-four poems. Given the vast body of work there is to choose from,
my selection is inevitably partial, in both senses of the word. My

choice of material was intuitive, but as I worked on the book, as the book came together, it took on a specific character of its own. *Gold* highlights Rumi's rhapsodic, ecstatic side. *Water*, by contrast, is *Gold*'s moody cousin. In its pages, Love responds to and is born from the challenges of earthly existence.

Rumi was an ecstatic, but he was also a man of his time and world. As a child, he was exposed to both extreme beauty and brutality. When he was around eleven years of age, he and his family left their home in present-day Afghanistan and began a ten-year journey through what are now Iran, Iraq, Syria, Saudi Arabia, and Turkey, sometimes traveling with a caravan of up to three hundred people, sometimes fleeing towns ahead of the Mongolian army which was pushing across Asia and wreaking havoc on village after village. We can imagine Rumi traveling through majestic landscapes of desert, mountain, meadow, and forest, inhaling the scent of wildflowers, gazing at skies brimming with stars, waking to choirs of birds, and wandering through rose gardens, cypress groves, peach orchards, and bazaars of aromatic spices, all of which make their way into his poetry. In one ear, he would have heard folktales, poems, scripture, and the lively banter of the caravan; and in the other, news of the atrocities and panic sweeping the land as Genghis Khan's armies invaded nearby towns, massacred inhabitants, and left behind smoldering ruins.

The son of an erudite Islamic theologian, Rumi was encouraged to pray, fast, and study scripture as well as mathematics, philosophy, literature, and the languages of Persian, Arabic, and Turkish, all of which shaped his worldview and eventually his poetry. Rumi would follow in his father's footsteps to become a theologian in Konya, offering sermons to thousands, until around the age of forty when Shams of Tabriz, an itinerant Sufi mystic, drew him from the pulpit into a life of poetry and music. Religious conservatives of the time were wary of music and sought to delimit its presence in daily life, but Shams embraced it as a portal to the divine. With Shams's guidance, Rumi became an avid practitioner of *sama*, as deep listening and whirling dance were called. "Music, the sweetest orator of all, / has climbed into the pulpit," he affirms in one of his poems. "I'll sell my tongue now / and buy a thousand ears." Music awakened Rumi's muse. During *sama* gatherings, while whirling to the beat of a drum, he improvised his poems, which friends hurriedly scribbled down.

Rumi brought everything he had learned and everything he had seen of the world to his poetry. He brought his ecstasy and despair, his wonder and frustration. Many of his poems are sung in praise of divine Love. Others describe the beauties and mysteries of the natural world. Others yet confront the tragic dimension of human life. In *Water*, for instance, we hear Rumi address the warmongers of his own time:

> What kind of lightning are you, setting farms on fire?
> What kind of cloud are you, raining down stones?
>
> What kind of hunter?
> Caught in your own trap—
> a thief stealing from your own house.

Rumi was very much aware of the disfiguring power of what Sufis call *nafs eh amaareh*—the imperious ego—one aspect of the transmutable *nafs*, or self. "Enthralled by stuff and status," prone to greed, a lust for dominion, narcissism, and even brutality, the imperious ego blocks out or, for all its bluster, hides fearfully from the divine. It is, Rumi often says, an "uncooked," immature aspect of human nature, and perhaps because it is all too fixated on hording worldly goods, it is all too tragically evident in worldly life, taking the reins time and again. A foundational assumption in Sufi philosophy is that the *nafs* is not a fixed, static entity but a work in progress, a malleable entity, compounded of desires and distractions, which needs to be directed into true awareness. If one has an active conscience, a willingness to examine oneself honestly, and a commitment to spiritual practice, Sufis suggest, evolution into a more compassionate, relaxed, loving, and selfless state of existence is possible. And this process, they believe, is life's most important and fruitful mission. As Shams said, "Souls

come to Earth to ripen . . . to attain the true wealth of maturity . . .
the *nafs* has to evolve, this is the only way . . ."

Throughout his poetry, Rumi describes his own transformation
and encourages ours while questioning the value system that puts
plunderers on pedestals, prioritizes material gain over spiritual con-
nection, and champions control over others rather than mutual ful-
fillment. In the process he redefines maturity, wealth, success. For
Rumi the true king is not an authoritarian, lost in ego, devoid of
conscience, wreaking havoc on the world, but Love's servant, a gener-
ous, selfless force, "nourishing as mother's milk." "Master," he says,
"I'll leave you [in the fire] / till you're cooked, / till you're no longer
a slave to your mind, / till you're its master."

In *Water*, the word "Love" appears 96 times. An intangible force
with a very tangible impact, Love takes on many forms in Rumi's
poetry. Most often he speaks of what the Greeks call *agape*, a bound-
less, divine Love, and less often of *eros* or romantic love. Sometimes
there is no distinction between the two, and sometimes how we ap-
proach one opens the way to the other. In the poem that begins,
"Tomorrow I'll visit Love's tailor," Rumi notes the ephemeral nature
of romantic love, visiting the tailor in his "robe of melancholy, passion,
entanglements, and infatuations." The tailor "snips at it. / He snips
away one lover, / stitches in another. // This seam might hold. / This
seam might split. / I give my heart anyway." Knowing the risk and
loving anyway, he comes to know divine union. Whether this or that
connection endures or not, a larger Love, a shoreless Ocean of Love,
a Oneness continues to beckon and is ours to experience if only we
allow ourselves to.

In Rumi's poetry, this capital-L Love incarnates itself in all sorts
of ways. Sometimes Love is *aabeh hayat*—the water of life, a force
that bubbles up from the depths of the soul and flows through us,
watering the ground within and between us, ensuring that gardens
rather than battlefields emerge. Sometimes Love is a fire burning
away egoic narratives and projections that obscure our sense of inter-
connection and keep us separate. Love is a stream and a shoreless
ocean, wine and bread, a teacher and friend—"its face, a torch, filling

the house with light." It is warmth and civility. It is our ultimate home, "Wherever [we] go, it goes with [us]." Love, challenges us, wakes us from our slumber, "illuminates our blind eyes," "washing off the weight of days," "arriving from no side" and standing "on every side." Love is a 360-degree embrace of creation, a compassionate acceptance of what is, and also a force that drives us to discern and refine, creating more welcoming worlds within and without us. Love is our unobscured essence, at the root of the root of all creation, a force that brings life into existence and sets all particles whirling. Above all, Love is a practice. "Child of flesh and bone, you are a child of soul. / Love is your trade, your mission, your calling. / Why do you busy yourself with so many other tasks?"

Rumi is rooting for us. His poetry is filled with startling leaps of imagery and thought, praise and critique, confessions and invitations, and through it all, his concern for humanity is palpable and his central commitment—human liberation through the cultivation of Love—unwavering. His poems are ravishing and rapturous, knotty and demanding. As I can say from my own experience of many years, they do not let you go. Rumi is a dazzler and he is also a good friend. In the midst of life's challenges, his lines are lifelines.

—HALEH LIZA GAFORI

YOU SHOW your face, your flushed face,
and stones spin with joy.
Once again, for the sake of awestruck lovers,
lift the veil from your face, speak out loud,
so learning and logic lose their way,
so men of reason shatter their culture of unreasonable reason,
so water, reflecting you, becomes the jewel,
so fire retires from war.

When I see your beauty, when I see your virtue,
I don't need those two or three hanging lanterns,
I don't need the moon.
The old rusty heavens are no mirror for your face.
You breathe in, you exhale, and from the tied up, tightfisted world,
a new world is born.

Venus, you long for the eyes of Mars to gaze upon you?
Oh, come on. Play your harp. Sing your song.

MY HEART breaks when I look out
on the old turning wheel of the world—
the trickery, snares, and deception.

My heart breaks when I see pain
planted in the soil.
What will it yield but more pain?

What the world has called work,
I work hard not to do.

———

Man, man, man,
what kind of lightning are you, setting farms on fire?
What kind of cloud are you, raining down stones?

What kind of hunter?
Caught in your own trap—
a thief stealing from your own house.

You're sixty years old, you're seventy years old,
and you're still uncooked?
Still won't let Love's flames near,
won't let them burn you up?

Enthralled by stuff and status,
the crown, the turban, the king's beard—
thorns pricking your hands,

but where is your flower?

Gazing in the mirror,
you tilt your hat like a crescent moon—
but where is your light?

———

If once, for one day, you would sense the Beloved,
sense the Beloved's boundless Love,
you'd be a friend, a good friend.

I swear to the pure essence of the Love that loves us all,
if you let it intoxicate you—
kindness will reign,
benevolence will reign.

Love is your true prince, your true sheik.
Take a step towards your true master,
and you're no longer a horseman in an army,
you're the head of the cavalry.

Hold onto Love's hand. Seek Love's aid.
Feel its warmth. Nothing else will save you
from the ache of separation.

On a desolate night, remember Love.
Feel dawn breaking within.
How can night persist under a rising sun?

While you sleep, Love sits at your bedside
praying for you, weeping for you.

If I say more, the world will burn.

IF YOU don't know what Love is,
ask the desolate night,
ask unkissed lips and a sallow face
what they miss.

Still water tells stories of the moon and stars.
Bodies give body to intellect and soul.

Schoolbooks can't teach us
what Love teaches us—
grace, warmth, civility,

their countless ways.

I TRAVELED to every city.
There was none like the city of Love.

The city of Love?
I didn't know what it was.
I didn't know what I was missing.

Young and callow,
I ran from one city to another.
All I knew was a searing loneliness.

I didn't give Love a thought.
I walked straight out of its honeyed fields,
and like a beast,
grazed on whatever grass I could find.

I hungered for onions and leeks,
not quail, not honey, not manna.
How could I long for what I hadn't tasted?

Among souls, I was a soul alone,
a restless heart with no wings.

A flower has no tongue yet it tastes the rain.
A flower has no throat yet it drinks the rain.
So I tasted and drank the wine of kindness and laughter.
Without my knowing, without my doing.
it seeped into me.

Love called out to my soul,
come in, come close, I've built a house for you.
It won't be free of sorrow or trial.
Come anyway.

No, I said. I won't enter!
I resisted time and again.
I ripped off my clothes,
wailing in defiance.

Come or go, Love told me,
I am here, closer to you than the vein in your neck.

Then came the enchantment, toying, sweet words—
the magic of the bounding world.
Who am I not to be lured?

And who am I when Love obliterates the I
I thought I was,
drawing me from one path, leading me on another?

I could tell you,
but every time I get to this point,
the tip of my pen breaks.

MY HEART is a pen in your hand,
Beloved.

Write x tonight, y tomorrow,
sharpen the reed, hone your love letters, prescriptions, and odes.
I surrender to you.
You know me better than I do.

Dip me in the well—
get ink on my face, get ink in your hair.
Shake me. Put me to work.

One page from you has an edge so sharp,
it cuts off the world's head.
Now it can think with its heart.

The power of your pen matches your grace.
When Mars and Saturn conjoin, disaster strikes.
One page from you reverses the spell.

Doctor, you know what ails us.
Your words are the cure.

This pen feels no pride or shame.
It doesn't applaud or lash itself.
It knows it traverses the unknown.

The mind can't contain these paradoxes—
how the pen surrenders form to the formless,
giving the formless form.

RESTLESS HEART, tell me,
what are you made of?
Are you fire, water, human, angel?

From what direction have you arrived?
What fed you? Where did you graze?

Why do you leap toward non-existence—
toward annihilation and union?
Tell me what you know of it.

And why aim for my undoing?
Why uproot me,
why abandon reason,
why tear off your veil?

Wary of emptiness, every animal, every being avoids it,
except you.
You carry all your belongings into the void—
why?

Warm with fever, urgent, drunk, and in ruin, you go.
When will you stop and take some advice?
When will flirtatious eyes stop stealing you away?

You are a torrent of water flowing
from the mountaintop of the world toward the Ocean beyond place,
faster than I can breathe one breath.

You are the rose and the narcissus,
wide-eyed and fragrant,
intoxicating the lily and the cypress.

The whole garden and the whole season of spring
are bewildered by you.
What breeze touches you, they ask,
what breeze carries you off?

WORLD OF water and mud,
ever since I've known you,
I've known trial, tribulation, and torment.

You are a pasture for grazing donkeys,
not the abode of Jesus.
What am I doing in a pasture for grazing donkeys?

Why am I here?

World of water and mud,
you tied my hands and feet—why?

So I notice my hands and feet?
So I cherish them, untie them,
meet my liberator?

Only when the feast was spread
did you pour the fresh water.
Only when the feast was spread
did we taste the sweet water.

World of water and mud,
God called you a cradle.

Infant blossom, tell me,
how do you mature so fast?

                    The breeze touches me and I open.
                    Petals fall. Fruit ripens.

While here I am,

lifting my arms like a tree to the sky,
praising the One who made the sky,

but why insist on above and below
when my Source dwells in every here and every there?
Why ask where of everywhere?

Turn off the tongue. Turn off the mind.
Enter nothingness.

See things through nothing's eyes.

LIKE THE reed,
stripped of its tassels
and hollowed out,

we are headless,
empty enough to carry the music
that wants to move through us.

LAST NIGHT in my dream,
I saw my hunger. I saw my need.
I saw an emptiness only God can fill.

Enchanted by the beauty of this poverty,
I nearly fainted.

Enchanted by its perfection,
I lay awestruck till dawn.

This poverty is a mine of rubies.
Its red glow drapes me in silk.

SEEKERS ON a pilgrimage
to the house of God,
where are you going?
Where are you?

Your Beloved is here. Come back.
Your Beloved lives next door.
Your Beloved is right behind the wall.

Why are you wandering
round and round, lost in the desert?

Look beyond form.
Look into the faceless face of Love.
You are that Love.
You are the house—the dwelling place of Love—
and its maker.

You've traveled ten times to see the house of God.
You've described it in detail,
all its exquisite features.

Now tell me about the God inside.
For once, enter your own house.
Climb to the roof.

If you saw the garden, where are the flowers?
If you swam from God's sea, where is your soul's pearl?

Searching for treasure,
you've endured so much trouble.
Hear this truth—

you are the treasure
and the veil hiding it.

TO BROOD is to wander through a grove
where one sheep strays
and a hundred wolves follow.

Why did I make brooding my vocation
when awe was an option?

Thought spinner,
mull the wine of wonder.

I TASTED selflessness.
I hunger for more of it.

I tell your Love-drunk eyes,
I want to see like you, to shine like you,
to have your unmuddied sight—
that's what I long for.

A crown, a throne—I don't need them.
To bow to the ground, to serve Love—
that's what I long for.

A breeze wafts in from the East.
To inhale its fragrance, to confide in a friend—
that's what I long for.

Love, I am wax, waiting for your imprint.
Stamp me with your ring—
that's what I long for.

One moon hovers in the sky.
Another moon hides in the heart.
To live in its light—

that's what I long for.

THE WORLD'S river stopped flowing.
Season of warm rains, return.
Let the river flow again.

In the depths of the soul,
there is a gushing spring,
invisible to the eye.

Love, the water of life,
bubbles up from its depths—
no end to it.

Let Love's spring feed the world's river.

Where there is water, there is bread, my dear,
but you can't squeeze water from bread.

You are a guest on this earth, not a beggar.
Don't trade the water of your soul
for a morsel of bread.

End to end, the whole material world
is less than a single morsel.
Greed for crumbs dries up the river.

From a placeless place beyond earth and sky,
the water of life flows.
The sky, its pitcher. The earth, its cup.
The Source—a boundless Ocean.

Don't delay. Leap from the pond into the Ocean,
again and again.
There the fish is immortal.

The Ocean—the vision of that boundless Ocean—
restores light to our eyes.
Its waters run down the rooftop,
flow through the spout, and feed the garden.
Our faces, the blooming flowers.

Dates from the garden's palms
nourish the unborn savior
inside the holy mother.

At sea in that ocean,
you find ease, you find joy,
and the frantic watchman in you—
shaking his rattle and banging his stick—
falls silent.

Boundless waters guard the fish.

THE GARDEN'S scent is a messenger,
arriving again and again,
inviting us in.

Hidden exchanges, hidden cycles
stir life underground.
What stirs the life in you?
The garden asks.

The garden thrives.
Invites us to do the same.

Saplings break through darkness—
ladders set against the sky.
Mysteries ascend.

Lips of lilies open—
secrets whispered to the cypress.
Good news of spring blasts from the mouths of tulips,
among redbuds and willows,
nightingales perched like guards
over open coffers of nectar.

Leaves are tongues.
The fruit, a heart.
When the heart opens,
we know the tongue's worth.

NOT A lover?
Try spinning wool.

Still nothing?
Try a hundred jobs, a hundred crafts,
a hundred causes and paths.

If Love's wine hasn't seeped into your skull
by then,

go to the kitchen in Love's house
and lick the plates lovers left behind.

BATHED IN night and beaming,
an unexpected guest
entered our house.

Who is it? asked my heart.
The moon, said my soul.

Madmen that we were, we left
to scour the streets
in search of its bright face.

I'm right here, the moon said.
Inside!

We wandered farther and farther.
Deaf to its calls,
calling out in vain.

A drunk nightingale sings in our garden.
A drunk nightingale laments in our garden.
Who? Who? we call out like mourning doves,
hearing only our own one-note song.

At midnight, a crowd hunts for a thief
and a thief in the crowd shouts,
Yes, there's a thief among us!
It's him. It's her. It's me.

His voice, a lost thread
in a tangle of voices.

When you're searching for something,
search for the thief within—
master of distraction,

he pockets the moon and the nightingale.

Search for the Beloved,
closer to you than you.

Melt like snow.
Silent as a lily, the soul's tongue
springs from Love's soil.

BELOVED, WHEN your sweetness rains down
the price of rock candy plummets.

WHY ARE you ravaged by a single thought,
dragged down, sinking inward,
heavy with sorrow?

Piece by piece, I stitched you together.
Why has one doom-ridden thought
torn you into a hundred pieces?

You packed your belongings
and left the kingdom of my Love.
Now you wander alone.

I made the earth your cradle
but you won't relax.
You lie there, cold and wooden,
ill at ease.

I unleashed water from stone.
You marched off towards dry land.
Now you're hard as granite.

Child of flesh and bone, you are a child of soul.
Love is your trade, your mission, your calling.
Why do you busy yourself with so many other tasks?

In one house, you were wounded a hundred times.
You keep circling that house.
You keep eyeing the door.

In another house, you tasted a hundred kinds of sweetness.
You trusted none of them.
Bitter, you never grew sweet.

Dear one, I want to see you Love-drunk.
If my words make you vigilant and wary,
I'll say no more.

Here I am, gazing at you in silence.
Open your eyes to the Love in my eyes.
Drink it down.

TOMORROW I'LL visit Love's tailor.
My robe of longing,
a thousand yards long—
my robe of melancholy, passion, entanglements, and infatuations.

He snips at it.
He snips away one lover,
stitches in another.

This seam might hold.
This seam might split.
I give my heart anyway,

watching his miraculous hands
embroider silk with silk.

Separation might tear my robe to shreds.
His scissors might wound me—
I know. I give my heart anyway.

Amazed, I watch him add and subtract,
preserve or erase memories,
dyeing my thoughts with new colors.

My heart is his slate.
He scrawls down facts and figures,
measurements and names.

He multiplies me by another,
and proves what?
One times one is one?

He divides us,
scatters us in the sea, and rejoins us.
Each drop—one with the shoreless One.

We are sum, product, quotient, difference—
no matter.
His arithmetic, his algebra
always yields the same result—
one and only One—

a marvel shattering thought.

SUN IN the heart, sun in the soul,
fill the house with light again.

Fill our friends with joy.
Blaze in the eyes of enemies.
Blind them till they see.

Rise over the mountain.
Ripen the grapes.
Make rubies out of stones.

Sun in the sky, sun in the heart,
doctor, beacon,
take our hands. Use our hands.
Cure the ill and ailing.

Make the gardens green again,
adorn farm and meadow
with every fruit and flower.

Criminal to let clouds hide you.

Unveil your face
and brighten our dim world.

YOU CAN'T put out a fire, dear boy,
with another fire.

You can't wash my heart's open wound
with another's blood.

LOVE, YOU stole my prayer beads
and gave me poetry.

You found me, hunched over, chanting,
"No strength but in ... No strength but in ..."
thumbing bead after bead, mouthing my repentance.
My heart wasn't in it.

Love, you picked me up.
You made me sing,
spout poetry, clap my hands.

I used to be ascetic and chaste,
denying myself delight—
a mountain, stolid and unmoving.

What mountain can withstand your winds?

If I am a mountain, your voice echoes off me.
If I am a piece of straw, I burn in your fire.

Love, the moment I saw you,
I was ashamed.
Who was I? Who wasn't I?
What in me was alive? What in me was dead?
Your flames consumed my questions
and my shame.

In that radiant void,
the soul is born and renewed.

We are blind men under a blue sky,
crouching in the road.
Love, your moon illuminates our blind eyes,
lighting up the whole sky.

Saints and prophets
move unrecognized through the market.
Unseen, the soul moves through the world.

Praising you, we praise ourselves.
Whoever praises the sun
praises the eyes that see the sun.

Praise is an ocean.
Our words, a boat on the waves.

Tell me I was sleeping.
Tell me my eyes are stained with sleep.
I won't grieve. I'm awake now,
no shame for having slept.

Tender waves carry us.

GIVE THE musicians honey,
God, God, God.
Give the drummers iron hands.

They devoted their hands and feet to Love.
Give strength and health to their hands and feet.

Praising sound, praising creation,
they sow joy.
Praise their efforts.
Applaud the harvest.

Fill their cups at streams flowing through paradise.
Their melodies water our thirsty hearts.

In their longing, doves coo, singers chant—
the empty sky sings.

Build the musicians a sturdy tower,
stone upon stone, grace upon grace.

WHAT IS *sama*?
Sama is deep listening.
Sama is whirling dance.

In *sama,*
hidden corners of the heart
send wordless messages,
soothing the exiled heart.

Intelligence is a tree.
In *sama,* you hear the breeze in its branches.
You hear the branches bloom.

Listen to the musicians.
Listen with your heart.
Listen with your skin.
Doors open.

When melodies flood our ears,
scorpions in the mind drown.
Sorrow loses its sting.

Honeyed notes on a singer's lips
sweeten mine.

Round after round of joy
and no one has drunk
even a drop of wine.

Music, the sweetest orator of all,
has climbed into the pulpit.

I'll sell my tongue now
and buy a thousand ears.

SELFLESSNESS IS sky.
The bird of the heart
flies nowhere
but there.

YOU LONG to love? You ache for love?
Then pick up a dagger
and cut the throat of your inhibitions.

Don't be bashful.
Don't fear for your reputation.
You're damming the river.

Let the river flow where it will.

Listen to me with a clear mind.
There's no malice behind my words,
no hidden motive. No reason to fear what I ask.

Why did the Love-crazed lover go mad again and again,
tricking his mind a thousand times—
sometimes tearing off his clothes,
sometimes running to the mountains,
sometimes drinking poison,
sometimes asking to be nothing at all?

While you, dear one—
you walk along the shore, sidestepping the waves,
hitching your hem up so it doesn't get wet.

Plunge into the ocean.
This path of Love
overflows with ecstasy,
overflows with humility.

High waves wash up at your feet.
Kneel down. Kiss the ground.
Master, serve Love.

You'll be bezel and jewel
in a ring of shining lovers.

Look, the stars spin.
Seasons come and go.
The earth surrenders and suffers no loss.
What do you have to lose?

Let your whole body—
your hands, feet, heart, stomach—
every part of it,
submit to your soul.

Listen with your soul's ears.
Hear the clamor, hear the rapturous calls of lovers
echoing above the green earth, through the sky's blue dome.

Don't mute your drum.
Don't muffle the beat.
Walk bravely into the field and raise Love's flag.

When day arrives, night fades.
When the army of grace and benevolence arrives,
suffering is defeated.

Soul of souls, speak.
One by one, Love's secrets
slip from your mouth.

LOVE, YOUR waters, your melodies
whirl me and whirl me.
I'm the wheel in a mill.
Whirl me forever.

When my heart is troubled,
when my heart has fled,
keep me close.

No branch, no leaf, no piece of straw drawn to amber
will move without a breeze.
Unless desire stirs it, nothing in this world will dance.

Every element, every particle of every element
is a whirling lover, drunk on union.

The generous host lays out a feast.
Animals graze the sweet grass.

Didn't the ants tell secrets to Solomon?
Didn't the mountains sing
when David sang his songs of praise?

The sky is your lover.
Lay your head on its peaceful chest.
The sun is your lover. Drink its light.

Love moves through every mountain and field.
How else would green grow from earth's dark body?

I WASN'T always this Love-drunk,
this crazed, rapt, and enchanted.

Driven by reason, on guard,
I was a hunter—
calculating, charming, strategic.

The heart is a tender thing—
pulsing with blood, pulsing with life.
That wasn't me.

I wanted answers—
what is this, what is that,
and what will they be tomorrow?

Awe? I knew nothing of awe.
And the awestruck—
those free from the gnawing need to know the unknowable—
they didn't impress me.

Sit down with me. You're a smart one.
Consider what I was
and what I no longer am.

I wanted to be a kingpin,
top dog, bigger than big.

Like smoke, I climbed greedily,
going nowhere—
a crooked plume, wayward,
drifting over parched land,
thirsty for meaning.

I didn't know when Love hunts you down,
when you fall prey to Love,
you only rise higher.

Continuing my futile climb, I fell.
I fell,
like a gem, out of a pile of dirt—
not a hoarder of treasure.

Treasure.

ALL NIGHT, the sky wept
and I wept too,
all night.

The sky and I are of one creed.

Longing for the earth,
the sky weeps,
the sky laughs.

Perfume of tear-soaked
log and leaf rises.

The sky's tears fall.
Wet violets bloom.

And a lover's tears?
What happens when they fall?
Kindness blooms.
Affection blooms.

The salt of tears sweetens our lips.

PURE SOUL, grief purifies you.
Sacred body, grief erodes you.

In the fire of Love where you burn,
your paradise is born.

DIDN'T I tell you
there's no need to search for me?
I am here, your friend, forever.

In this life, where the body perishes,
where the mind constructs mirage after mirage,
I am your water. I am your fountain of life—
refreshing you, restoring sight.
Didn't I tell you?

If you turn from me in anger,
if you flee for a hundred thousand years,
you'll come back to me in the end.
I am your end. I am your beginning.

Didn't I promise you?
If bandits strip you bare,
if they steal your flames,
I am your blazing fire.

If you're a fish,
writhing on dry land,
I am your sea,
the calm waves that carry you.

Shiny images, flashy things lure everyone.
They can't give the contentment you seek.
Didn't I tell you?

I've built a home for you—
everything in its place.
Wherever you go, it goes with you.
Settle there.

Were you caught like prey?
Did you fall in a trap?
Didn't I tell you not to be fooled?
Come close.
I give you the power to fly.

Didn't I tell you?
Your heart is a lamp.
It lights your way home.
Your soul, divine.
It leads you back to me.

So I've told you,
and dear one,
I'll tell you again.

FRESH, BLISSFUL—the moment
we sat in the courtyard, you and me.
Two bodies, two faces, one soul, you and me.

The garden's murmurs, the garden's music,
the babbling brook of birdsong flows through us
like the water of life, we walk among roses, you and me.

The stars bend low to see us, we fill their eyes,
outshine the moon, you and me.

No me versus you here.
No me, me, me or you, you, you here.
We are free of gripes, free of nagging thoughts and delusions,
raucous laughter is here,
parrots drunk on celestial honey.

A stroke of magic that we are here,
while breathing the air of Baghdad's orchards,
while breathing the air of Khorasan's streams, you and me.

One form on earth, another in paradise,
eternal, in the land of honey, you and me.

HERE WE are today, caught in a whirlpool.
Let's see who stays afloat.

If waves high as camels flood the world,
waterbirds won't despair.

What better teacher than the high sea's heavy waves?
Like fish, our souls thrive,
our faces lit with gratitude.

In each mind, these winds stir up a different madness.
Give me the madness of the crazed, selfless lover,
pouring Love's wine, filling everyone's cup.
You can have the rest.

Yesterday, he spotted a band of Love-drunk seekers on the road.
He snatched their turbans and crowns.
Today, he fills our cups to the brim.
He can have our royal cloaks.

Envy of the moon and Jupiter,
hidden among us like a spirit,
gently you lead me on.
Will you ever tell me where we're going?

Wherever you go, you are with me.
You are my eyes, my clarity, my light.
Lead me where you wish—
to dissolution, to union, to ecstasy.

The world is our holy mountain.
We are seekers like Moses.

One glimpse of the divine,
and the mountain shatters—
emerald, amber, opal, and ruby light up our eyes.

If you want to see God,
gaze at the mountain.
We are drunk on the echoes in the valley.

Gardener, gardener, why stop us in our tracks?
If we stole your grapes, you can take our sack.

EVEN SPRING rains
can't draw green stalks
out of a stone.

A hard, sharp stone,
you broke hearts for years—
a barren life.

Be soil.
For once, try.
Color after color springs from soil.

WHEN WE die, we marry eternity.
The secret revealed:
God, us, all—One.

Sunlight shining through a carved stone screen
splits. You can count the beams
though the source is one sun.

You can count the grapes in a cluster
but not the grapes in wine.

The light inside the body flickers and dies.
The Source shines on, eternal.

God—Creator—Unfathomable One—
you grant us vision.

A bird with hungry eyes
is flying towards you.

THE DEAD all leave something behind.

Better a trail of good deeds
than a pile of coins.
The world remembers virtue—

and no one can steal it.

I'LL NEVER tire of you.
I'll never stop thirsting for you—
that's my only fault.

Wrap me in compassion, in your untiring compassion.
You are my haven, here and beyond.

I called on the water bearer again and again.
I drank from his jug. I drank from his waterskin.
I grew thirstier with every drink,
exhausting them all.

Smash the jug. Slash the waterskin.
Clear the path.
I'm heading for the boundless Ocean.

How long have my tears turned the earth to mud?
How long has my sadness darkened the sky with smoke?
How long has my broken heart grieved its brokenness?
How long have my lips complained to the King of kings?

Go to the Ocean.
Waves of purity, waves of serenity roll in.
Wash away my old self—
old home—
the old trap of my old ways.

Last night, in one great wave, the water of life
crashed in the courtyard of my house.
The flood swept my harvest away.

Smoke rose from my heart.
My grain and hay burned to ash.

I'm not grieving. Why should I grieve?
The halo around the moon is enough for me
and I can't eat sorrow.

Beloved,
you entered my heart, your image aflame.
Your fire blazed through my head,
burning my hat, my turban, my crown.

Listen, you said. Listen to the music.
Though you might lose what you call dignity,
though you might stain your reputation,
dance the whirling dance.

Beloved, your Love is my dignity.
Your Love is my honor.
Knowing you is enough.

The light of your midnight face
outshines the dawn.

I know the army of sadness is near,
but its sadness can't overtake me.
My army of yearning, my army of Love
has reached heaven.

My heart regrets every ode I write—
I've said too much, I know—

and then again the falcon dives down,
seizes my heart, urges me on.

I DRANK the soul's wine.
It set me ablaze.

Now like a moth, the sun
flutters around my fire.

YOU PLAY the strings of my heart.
You play a new chord—

light of mine, love of mine,
eyes of mine—

you are music—
the melodies, the fade-out,
and the memory of it all.

Each breath with you,
a new note, a new color.

Every chord you strum
lifts a curtain from my eyes,
waking me from oblivion,
from all my forgetting.

At night, alone, with my soul's swaying lanterns,
I'm astonished. Who are you—
both flame and fuel
keeping my flickering light alive?

Your songs tell me,
you are a body, you are a body.

If I am body, if I am heart, if I am soul,
I am happy you are the one
weaving me.

You are the cypress, the blooming lily and rose.
Everything blossoms in your presence,
why shouldn't I?

You shine through the windows of every house.
Why shouldn't I let your light in?

You are iron too, and boulder—
why shouldn't I know your quiet power?

AT SUNSET we pray.
The path of the senses closes.
The path to the unseeable opens.

Like a shepherd tending a flock,
the angel of sleep urges souls
through placeless meadows, gardens, cities.

Sleep wipes the slate clean.
Thousands of new faces and forms appear.
The wide-eyed soul watches in awe,

and perhaps it always dwells there,
where no memory persists,
where the bodiless body never tires.

The heart that trembles here
under the weight of possessions—
under the weight of their absence—

soars weightless there.

WON'T YOU praise Love?
Won't you praise its virtues, charms, allurements?

Love shows its face—
its warmth and mercy.
The torn world reunites.

Love, you are wine.
We are jugs.
You are water.
We are the stream.

Arriving from no side,
you stand on every side.

How then does my heart walk towards you?
How do my eyes find you?
What words can I say to draw words from your lips?

Love, what did you whisper in the ear of the heart
to make it bloom with laughter?

Melodies are pouring out of an empty reed,
honey is dripping from a hive—
what did you feed the musicians and bees
to make the honey so sweet?

What do you feed the mind to make a mind
kind, noble, eager to serve?

Everywhere, earth is vivid with your colors.
Wonder is struck with wonder.
The heart trembles in awe.

You are water flowing through heavy hearts,
washing off the weight of days.

THOUGH I appear to be walking through the alley of my beloved,
I am riding a green horse on the spinning wheel of the cosmos.

A hundred worlds traversed in one breath,
and I've taken only one step.

LOVER NEARS lover.
Closer and closer,
crazy with love.

Chains break.
Thought disintegrates.

Faces flushed with fire.
Where's the fault in that?
Love's flame reduces guilt to ash.

A hundred veils bury sight.
Like an arrow, a lover's glance
tears through them all.

Do you know that eager bird
inside a lover's heart,
pecking away at its shell,
ready to hatch?

The world is a tar pit.
Our feet are stuck in it.
Love's flames melt the tar.
We step free.

Shams, king and truth of Tabriz,
in your presence, my patience
is a tattered old shirt.

THE WHIRLING dance leaves the heart restless for more—
more music, more dance.

Lit by lightning, we flash like spring clouds.

Venus, you know this ecstasy.
Open your generous palms to the musicians.
Their hands—and drums—are spent!

LOVE IS full of baits and traps.
I swear by it anyway.

I'll travel all the way from Konya to Damascus
countless times for Love.

What's allowed? What's not allowed?
I don't ask. I swear by a Love
beyond prohibitions and permissions.

I swear by a gentle Love,
more tender than the Soul of souls.
This Love is my bread.
This Love is my wine.

People were spreading rumors.
Jealous people, they drove my beloved Shams from town.
When we searched for him and didn't find him,
they rejoiced.

Didn't they know my soul lives on Love's flames,
like a fire-eating salamander,
my soul feeds on Love's flames?

Isn't Love the crucible where my pennies turn to gold?
Doesn't Love pour the wine?
My body, its vessel.

Morning and night,
my hungover soul craves a sip.
Morning and night,
my soul finds its confidant in that Love,
trading secrets no poem, no language could ever convey.

Bring the wine—
not the wine of crushed grapes—
bring Love's wine.

Fill this empty cask.
Fill this empty house.
This lover is a beginner,
still uncooked.

Circumspect mind, suffering body—
take a rest.
Draw close to Love.
Let it challenge you.
Enjoy Love. Tremble with Love.

Steeped in that wine,
we find Shams, the king of Tabriz,
returning to greet us.

MASTER, YOUR head is swollen with fantasies.
One moment, you celebrate,
one moment, you sulk.

You're in the fire now. I'll leave you there
till you're cooked,
till you're no longer a slave to your mind,
till you're its master.

A GREAT Love settled across the land.
May it live on forever.

Cynics found faith.
May faith in Love live on forever.

In a land ravaged by its demons,
compassion, wisdom, and intelligence rose again.
May they lead us forever.

My friend broke my heart, slammed the door,
came back with compassion and remorse.
May the change of heart last forever.

You're all alone, savoring your wine,
a lonely pleasure.
Join us. Be our guest forever.

Like a torch, Love's face fills the house with light.
Cramped corners open to fields.
May the fields expand forever.

The grief-struck teach me.
The Love-drunk teach me.
Enthralled by their bravery, their joy, their triumph,
I cast off my chains.
May this freedom last forever.

Sweet lips draw music from a hollow reed.
Wind and sky sing.
May the music echo on.

The moon shines. Orchards bloom.
People find their souls.
May the blossoming go on forever.

Silence. Someone just tied the hands of my old life,
and I'm drunk on Love, thoughts stumbling.
Let thought stumble off forever.

LOVE FLOODS the eyes of the devoted
with tears of remorse,
washing the heart clear of grudges and denial.

Love dashes your face with the water of life,
urging you to leap from your slumber.

Rise up, take my cup, Love says,
drink eternity.

ON THE day I die,
when they carry me to my grave,
don't be so sure I'm dying to come back!

Don't weep for me, dear love.
Don't cry out, What a pity! How terrible!
You're gone. You're gone!

This leaving is an arrival,
a reunion.

Lower me into my grave
with no goodbye.

If the grave is a cage,
the soul flies free of it.

If the grave is a curtain,
gardens blossom beyond it.

When the sun and moon set,
they climb another sky.
When you see me going down,
see me rising.

A bucket disappears in the well
and comes up full.
A seed is buried in the ground.
A flower sprouts.

Why imagine another fate
for the seed of the human soul?

My mouth closes in this world
and opens in the other.

A shout of joy echoes
through the placeless sky.

YOUR FRAGRANT breeze is everywhere,
God.

Look at the people shuffling in,
their souls, headless and footless,
thirsty for you.

Nursed on your milk, nursed on your generosity,
but still fretful like infants waiting for their mothers.
All aching from separation, all longing for union.

Thirsting for you, they hear the call of the water bearer.

Every dawn, prayers rise with the sun.
Muslims, Jews, Christians call out.

Happy and blessed is the mind that hears
with the ear of the heart
invitations, calls for communion,
falling from the sky.

Clear your ears, clear your mind
of unkind, torturous words.
Hear the voice of heaven here.

If your eyes are polluted,
let your tears wash them.
The cure is in your tears.

I hear footsteps and bells,
a caravan from Egypt is approaching,
sweetness for the tongue and sweetness for the ears—
sugar and an eloquent king.

Silence.
Let the King finish the poem.

YOUR FACE enslaves kings
and your smile makes kings of slaves.

How long will you hide that smile?
Your face,
a bright, auspicious moon.

Teach the red rose how to laugh.
Wrap us in eternal grace.

The door to heaven closed
so someone like you would appear
and open it.

The whole caravan of drunk camels
longs for you to lead.
Let your hair loose, your curls lasso hearts,
your locks unlock the soul.

Today is the day for union—
why wait?
The Beloved is here.

The wounded lover aches,
the drum's skin is cold,
the reed cries out for your lips.

Beat a rhythm on that drum, breathe into the reed.
If the lute calls out, longing for you,
open your generous hand,
play the strings.

Don't fault the poem for remaining unfinished.
The bird of the imagination flies where it likes.

AT DAWN, the sea of honey spoke:
Open your eyes to wave on wave of honey.
Open your eyes to the poem.

When you fast,
drink the sound of water.
The sound does its work—

the sound of water lapping the shore,
the sound of water gurgling among rocks.

Deep listening does its work.
A babbling brook for thirsty seekers,
it gives you life.

Touched by the water of life, a bald head
sprouts locks of perfumed hair.
Mixed with this water,
wine clears the drunkard's head.
Be patient, you'll see.

You've emerged from me, says the water,
you'll return.

I WAS dead. I came to life.
I was tears. Now I'm laughter.

Love found me, shook me,
woke me to the eternal Love within.

My eyes are sated with appearances.
My eyes have seen all that eyes can see.
My soul is bold. It leads.

With the shining warmth of Venus,
with the courage of a lion,
I follow.

———

Long ago, Shams found me.
Long ago, Shams told me,

you're not crazy enough.
You don't belong in this house.

So I left. I lost my mind.
I came back, bound in chains.

You're still tied up? Shams said.
That's not the crazy I'm talking about.
Go. You're not one of us.

So I left again. I got drunk
and came back, overflowing with glee.

You're not drunk on Love, Shams said.
You're not dead drunk.
Come back when ecstasy has soaked you to the bone.

His face shined with life.
I fell dead at his feet.

That's clever, Shams said,
but you're drunk on doubt and delusion,
not on Love.

Dumbstruck,
I gave up. I hid from all.

You can't hide, Shams said.
You're the idol to your worshippers.
You're the candle lighting their way.

I'm no idol. I'm no candle, I said.
I'm the scattering of smoke.

But you're a preacher, a sheik,
a torchbearer, a leader.

No, I am your servant, I said.

My servant?
Well, you have your own wings and feathers.
You don't need mine to fly.

Longing for his wings,
I fell, plucked and wingless.

Love spoke in a new voice:
no need to trudge and toil.
I am here, walking towards you
in kindness and grace.

Love spoke in its ancient voice:
Stay close to me. Settle here.
So I did. So I found peace.

———

Beloved,
you are a fountain of sunlight.
I am the shade of a willow.

When your rays reach me,
striking my head, caressing my brow,
I fall. I melt away.

You tore open my heart.
Now it shines with a new luster.
It spins the finest silks.
I am a stranger to the old rags.

Arrogant and boastful in my youth,
I was a slave to my mind,
a stableman led by a donkey.
Now I'm a king.

———

I thank you as the dark earth thanks the celestial wheel.
Only by your circling gaze do shadows lift,
do I bathe in light.

I thank you as the heavens thank the creator and the angels.
Only by your grace and generosity,
do I know bounty, do I pour forth light.

I thank you as the mystic thanks revelation.
Only by your wisdom,
do I reach the heights of a star in the seventh sky.

I am born from you, O celebrated moon.
Look at me and see yourself.

Watered by your laughter,
I am a garden of laughing flowers.

Like a chess player,
I make my moves in silence.
In the company of the King,
I am reborn to bliss.

WHEN I leave this body,
people will ask—
what did he do with his life?

I knew you, Beloved.
That was enough.

ACKNOWLEDGMENTS

FIRST and foremost, I want to thank the line of women storytellers in my family, and specifically my great-grandmother Bagum and my mother, Marzie T. Nejad. Visibly and invisibly, they passed down a love of language, an impulse to speak aloud, and a treasure chest of stories to me, stories which wind through Molana Rumi's poetry. As I worked on the poems in *Gold* and *Water,* my mother and I often recited the Persian text together, marveled at Rumi's genius, discussed elusive lines, debated meanings, researched words, and felt ourselves nourished, uplifted, and changed by the poems. I am forever grateful for her vast knowledge, care, generosity, and desire to dive into Rumi's sea with me, anytime I asked.

Another central figure in the creation of these two volumes is my editor, Edwin Frank. His attention, intelligence, talent, and humor have been a gift in my life, and neither I nor the books would be the same without him. Endless gratitude to Edwin.

Many thanks to the team at MacDowell for giving me time and space to develop and refine *Water,* and to the team at New York Review Books for believing in the work, and for making and distributing such beautiful books. It's an honor to be included in the series and to work with you all.

Thank you to the professors and coordinators at universities, including Stanford University, Swarthmore College, Sarah Lawrence College, Colorado State University, Saint Joseph's University, Columbia University, Houghton College, and St. Olaf College, who have presented my translations of Rumi's poetry to students and/or invited me to visit and share the work myself. It has been an utter joy to offer these poems and commune with faculty and students.

The teams at the Academy of American Poets and the Poetry Society of New York have done so much to get more poetry into our minds and hearts. I thank them for that, and for inviting me to share my translations in seminars on- and offline. Thank you to the editors at *Harvard Review* and *The Brooklyn Rail* for being the first to publish some of the poems in this volume.

Heartfelt thanks to all the writers, artists, musicians, friends, and family members who inspire me every single day. I adore you. You are lifelines—artistic prowess, skill, intelligence, and/or kindness incarnate.

And finally, immense gratitude to my father, Iraj Gafori, a gentleman, scholar, doctor, humanist, lover of nature, lover of literature, and the first person to recite Molana's poetry to me. I inherited awe from him. May he rest and soar in peace.

INDEX OF POEMS

Excerpts or complete Ghazals (G) and Rubaiyat/Quatrains (R) numbered according to Foruzanfar's edition of the *Divan-e Shams-e Tabrizi*, unless otherwise indicated.

OTHER NEW YORK REVIEW CLASSICS

For a complete list of titles, visit www.nyrb.com.

RUMI Gold; translated by Haleh Liza Gafori
FELIX SALTEN Bambi; or, Life in the Forest
JONATHAN SCHELL The Village of Ben Suc
GERSHOM SCHOLEM Walter Benjamin: The Story of a Friendship
DANIEL PAUL SCHREBER Memoirs of My Nervous Illness
JAMES SCHUYLER Alfred and Guinevere
JAMES SCHUYLER What's for Dinner?
LEONARDO SCIASCIA The Day of the Owl
LEONARDO SCIASCIA Equal Danger
LEONARDO SCIASCIA The Moro Affair
LEONARDO SCIASCIA To Each His Own
LEONARDO SCIASCIA The Wine-Dark Sea
VICTOR SEGALEN René Leys
ANNA SEGHERS The Dead Girls' Class Trip
VICTOR SERGE The Case of Comrade Tulayev
VICTOR SERGE Conquered City
VICTOR SERGE Last Times
VICTOR SERGE Memoirs of a Revolutionary
VICTOR SERGE Midnight in the Century
VICTOR SERGE Notebooks, 1936–1947
VICTOR SERGE Unforgiving Years
ELIZABETH SEWELL The Orphic Voice
ANTON SHAMMAS Arabesques
CHARLES SIMIC Dime-Store Alchemy: The Art of Joseph Cornell
CLAUDE SIMON The Flanders Road
MAY SINCLAIR Mary Olivier: A Life
TESS SLESINGER The Unpossessed
WILLIAM GARDNER SMITH The Stone Face
VLADIMIR SOROKIN Blue Lard
VLADIMIR SOROKIN Red Pyramid: Selected Stories
VLADIMIR SOROKIN Telluria
JEAN STAFFORD Boston Adventure
GEORGE R. STEWART Fire
GEORGE R. STEWART Storm
STENDHAL The Life of Henry Brulard
ADALBERT STIFTER Motley Stones
HOWARD STURGIS Belchamber
ITALO SVEVO As a Man Grows Older
ITALO SVEVO A Very Old Man
HARVEY SWADOS Nights in the Gardens of Brooklyn
A.J.A. SYMONS The Quest for Corvo
MAGDA SZABÓ The Fawn
SUSAN TAUBES Lament for Julia
ELIZABETH TAYLOR Mrs Palfrey at the Claremont
TEFFI Other Worlds: Peasants, Pilgrims, Spirits, Saints
TATYANA TOLSTAYA The Slynx
TATYANA TOLSTAYA White Walls: Collected Stories
EDWARD JOHN TRELAWNY Records of Shelley, Byron, and the Author
LIONEL TRILLING The Liberal Imagination
LIONEL TRILLING The Middle of the Journey
YŪKO TSUSHIMA Woman Running in the Mountains
IVAN TURGENEV Fathers and Children
IVAN TURGENEV Virgin Soil